World Almanac® Library of American Immigration

Mexican Americans

Scott Ingram

Curriculum Consultant: Michael Koren,
Social Studies Teacher, Maple Dale School, Fox Point, Wisconsin

WORLD ALMANAC® LIBRARY

Please visit our web site at: www.garethstevens.com
For a free color catalog describing World Almanac® Library's
list of high-quality books and multimedia programs,
call 1-800-848-2928 (USA) or 1-800-387-3178 (Canada).
World Almanac® Library's fax: (414) 332-3567.

Library of Congress Cataloging-in-Publication Data

Ingram, Scott.
    Mexican Americans / by Scott Ingram.
        p. cm. — (World Almanac Library of American immigration)
    Includes bibliographical references and index.
    ISBN-10: 0-8368-7316-5 — ISBN-13: 978-0-8368-7316-0 (lib. bdg.)
    ISBN-10: 0-8368-7329-7 — ISBN-13: 978-0-8368-7329-0 (softcover)
    1. Mexican Americans—History—Juvenile literature. 2. Mexican Americans—
Social conditions—Juvenile literature. 3. Immigrants—United States—History—Juvenile
literature. 4. Mexico—Emigration and immigration—History—Juvenile literature.
5. United States—Emigration and immigration—History—Juvenile literature. I. Title.
II. Series.
E184.M5I46   2007
973'.0046872—dc22   2006005387

First published in 2007 by
World Almanac® Library
A member of the WRC Media Family of Companies
330 West Olive Street, Suite 100
Milwaukee, WI 53212, USA

Produced by Discovery Books
Editor: Jim Mezzanotte
Designer and page production: Sabine Beaupré
Photo researcher: Rachel Tisdale
Maps and diagrams: Stefan Chabluk
Consultant: Amy Bauman
World Almanac® Library editorial direction: Mark J. Sachner
World Almanac® Library editor: Carol Ryback
World Almanac® Library designer: Scott M. Krall
World Almanac® Library art direction: Tammy West
World Almanac® Library production: Jessica Morris

Picture credits: Cover: Richard Cummins/CORBIS; title page, p. 27: Dorothea Lange/U. S. Office
of War Information/Library of Congress; p. 5: U. S. Customs & Border Protection; p. 7:
CORBIS; p. 8: Paul Humphrey/CFW Ltd; p. 9: Library of Congress; p. 11: U. S. Office of War
Information/Library of Congress; p. 12: U. S. Customs & Border Protection; p. 13: James
Tourtellotte/ U. S. Customs & Border Protection; p. 14: Bettmann/CORBIS; p. 16: Leonard
Nadel/National Museum of American History/Reuters/CORBIS; p. 17: Library of Congress;
p. 18: U. S. Office of War Information/Library of Congress ; p. 19: Harry Pennington/ Keystone/Getty
Images; p. 21: Kevin Lamarque/Reuters/CORBIS; p. 22: C. Moore/CORBIS; p. 25: Bettmann/CORBIS;
p. 26: Steve Crise/CORBIS; p. 28: Bettmann/CORBIS; p. 29: Bettmann/ CORBIS; p. 31: Tim
Graham/Evening Standard/Getty Images; p. 33: Bettmann/ CORBIS; p. 34: Gilles Mingasson/
Getty Images; p. 35: Hector Mata/AFP/Getty Images; p. 36: Robert Pirillo/Ovoworks /Time & Life
Pictures/Getty Images; p. 39: Joe Raedle/ Newsmakers/ Getty Images; p. 41: Alison Wright/CORBIS;
p. 42: J. Emilio Flores/Getty Images

Printed in the United States of America

2 3 4 5 6 7 8 9 10 09 08 07

Contents

Front cover: Dancers in San Diego, California, during a festival on Cinco de Mayo, a Mexican holiday.

Title page: Mexicans wait at a U.S. center for new immigrants in El Paso, Texas, in 1938.

Introduction

The United States has often been called "a nation of immigrants." With the exception of Native Americans—who have inhabited North America for thousands of years—all Americans can trace their roots to other parts of the world.

Immigration is not a thing of the past. More than seventy million people came to the United States between 1820 and 2005. One-fifth of that total—about fourteen million people—immigrated since the start of 1990. Overall, more people have immigrated permanently to the United States than to any other single nation.

Push and Pull

Historians write of the "push" and "pull" factors that lead people to emigrate. "Push" factors are the conditions in the homeland that convince people to leave. Many immigrants to the United States were—and still are—fleeing persecution or poverty. "Pull" factors are those that attract people to settle in another country. The dream of freedom or jobs or both continues to pull immigrants to the United States. People from many countries around the world view the United States as a place of opportunity.

Building a Nation

Immigrants to the United States have not always found what they expected. People worked long hours for little pay, often doing jobs that others did not want to do. Many groups also endured prejudice.

In spite of these challenges, immigrants and their children built the United States of America, from its farms, railroads, and computer industries to its beliefs and traditions. They have enriched American life with their culture and ideas. Although they honor their heritage, most immigrants and their descendants are proud to call themselves Americans first and foremost.

The Mexican American Story

Mexican Americans have a unique place in U.S. history. Long before there was a nation called the United States, Mexicans lived within the country's present-day borders. In the 1800s, the United States expanded to include land that had been part of Mexico. Many people of Mexican descent became Americans simply because the United States grew to include them. Today, the two countries share a long border.

Mexico has long been a poor country with many problems. Since the early 1900s, poverty and violence have driven thousands of Mexicans north to the United States. Each year, about three hundred thousand Mexican immigrants arrive legally in the United States, while many more cross the border illegally. More than twenty million people of Mexican descent now live in the United States. They have played important roles in the country's economy, and they have reached positions of influence in all levels of government. Mexican culture in the United States, from language to food to music, has had a major influence on the American way of life.

▼ Every day, long lines of cars in Mexico wait to cross the U.S. border.

CHAPTER 1

Life in the Homeland

Mexico is a nation of more than one hundred million people that is about three times the size of Texas. It is a mix of different peoples and different cultures with a long, proud history. From 1521 to 1821, Mexico was a colony called "New Spain," which was ruled by the powerful Spanish empire. Long before Spanish conquistadors arrived, however, Mexico was home to several great empires, such as the Olmecs, Maya, and Aztecs. Today, most Mexicans can trace their ancestry to the peoples of these ancient empires.

Spanish Influence

In 1519, Spanish conquistador Hernán Cortés landed on Mexico's Yucatan peninsula. Cortés arrived with about five hundred men. At that time, it is believed that about twenty-five million people lived in the region that is now Mexico. In 1521, Cortés and his men conquered Tenochtitlan. This huge city, located on the site of present-day Mexico City, was the capital of the Aztec empire. Cortés managed to conquer many people with a small army, but

◀ Mexico is in southwestern North America. Its border with the United States is 2,000 miles (3,219 kilometers) long.

▲ Before the Spanish arrived, Mexico was home to several civilizations. The Mayans built this pyramid, at Chichén Itzá, more than fifteen hundred years ago.

he had a powerful ally: disease. The region's natives had no immunity from European diseases, such as smallpox. In less than two years, smallpox killed more than half of the people in Tenochtitlan. It was the same story across all of Mexico. By 1620, about 97 percent of the native people in Mexico had been wiped out by conquest and disease.

More Spanish explorers followed Cortés, and the colony of New Spain was established. Soldiers who arrived from Spain often married native women. Their children—a mix of European and Native Indian descent—became known as mestizos. People born in Mexico who only had Spanish ancestors became known as criollos. The mestizos eventually became the largest ethnic group in Mexico. Today, most Mexicans are mestizos.

The Catholic Church played a big role in New Spain, just as it did in Spain. Catholic priests often traveled with Spanish explorers. The priests established missions, which became larger settlements. By the late 1700s, Spanish settlements had been established in the modern-day states of Texas, New Mexico, Arizona, and California.

Independence and Conflict

By the early 1800s, New Spain extended as far north as present-day central California. In 1821, the colony won independence from Spain and became the nation of Mexico. Then, in 1836, Mexico lost a war with Americans who had settled in Texas, which had been part of Mexico. Texas became independent, and the river called the Rio Grande became the border between Mexico and Texas. By 1846, Texas was part of the United States, and war once again broke out.

▲ The Alamo, in San Antonio, Texas, was once a Spanish mission. Although Mexican troops defeated Texans at the Alamo, Texas still won its independence.

Mexico was defeated in this conflict, known as the Mexican-American War (1846–1848). Under the treaty of Guadalupe Hidalgo that ended the war, Mexico gave up most of its territories north of the Rio Grande. The U.S. government agreed, however, to allow Mexicans in those regions to become U.S. citizens and to retain ownership of any land they had purchased.

By 1860, civil war had broken out in Mexico. On one side were the criollos, who held most of the country's power and wealth. On the other side were the mestizos, the poorest people in Mexican society. Although the criollos won the war, decades of fighting had made Mexico weak, and it was invaded by French forces. The French eventually left Mexico. In 1876, Porfirio Díaz, a general who had helped defeat the foreign invaders, became the president of Mexico.

Mexican Revolution

For more than thirty years, President Díaz ruled Mexico with almost total control. Some Mexicans admired him because he had brought stability and peace to their country. Díaz, however, allowed foreign investors and his own criollo supporters to control much of the country's natural resources. He also gave wealthy Mexicans the rights to farmland that traditionally belonged to local villages. By 1910, a few hundred wealthy investors

"As a third generation Mexican American, I try . . . to . . . understand the plight of many immigrants these days. But I . . . will never understand how difficult things were back in the day. I am so grateful to those before me who had the vision, drive and work ethic to take a brave chance in a new country and strive for a better life. Today I am middle school teacher."

Ricardo Calzada, 2005

▲ The Federales, shown here at a meeting in 1914, were one of many groups fighting for control of Mexico during the Mexican Revolution.

owned more than 30 percent of Mexico's farmland. More than half of all Mexicans were forced to work on large farms, called haciendas, where they labored long hours for little pay.

In 1910, unrest spread among the mestizo peasants. Two men, Emiliano Zapata and Pancho Villa, formed private rebel armies that fought the Mexican government. This violent conflict, known as the Mexican Revolution, continued for almost twenty years. It resulted in the first wave of Mexican immigration. Between 1910 and 1930, about seven hundred thousand legal immigrants came to the United States from Mexico.

More Push and Pull

The next wave of immigration began in 1942, during World War II. At that time, Mexico had many unemployed people. With the war on, the United States needed workers. The two countries agreed to a program that allowed Mexican workers into the United States temporarily to harvest crops and work in factories. It was called the "bracero" program, after the Mexican word for worker, *bracero*. The program ended in the 1960s. By then, it had drawn millions of Mexican laborers to the United States, and about two hundred thousand of them stayed permanently.

In the second half of the twentieth century, Mexico faced constant economic problems. It also suffered from natural disasters. In 1985, for example, central Mexico experienced two major earthquakes. Between five thousand and ten thousand people died, and more than three hundred thousand people lost their homes. The combination of economic depression and natural disaster began the third wave of immigration that continues to this day.

CHAPTER 2

Emigration

More than one million people died in battles over land rights during the Mexican Revolution. The violence forced thousands of Mexicans to cross the border into Texas across the shallow Rio Grande. Thousands more emigrated to California. They walked long distances to the border city of Tijuana, Mexico, and then crossed the U.S. border into San Diego, California. It is estimated that nearly ten percent of Mexico's total population emigrated between 1910 and 1924. Large numbers of Mexicans continued to emigrate through the rest of the 1920s.

Becoming a Bracero

In 1942, Mexican workers began entering the United States through the bracero program. The majority of these workers were skilled farm laborers who came from productive agricultural regions in Mexico. By American standards, they were poor, but in Mexico, they were considered middle class. In the hope of earning "riches" in the United States, they stopped working their own land and headed north to Chihuahua City, the capital of the Mexican state of Chihuahua, which borders Texas.

The workers got off a train and stood in line at the *trocadero* next to the railroad station. The trocadero was an office run by Americans who interviewed workers and asked to see the palms of their hands. Men with "soft" hands—proof that they were not used to hard physical labor—were denied entry. Workers who were chosen signed contracts and had their pictures taken. From Chihuahua City, they were taken by truck to Ciudad Juárez, across the border from El Paso, Texas.

In Ciudad Juárez, the bracero workers waited, often for several days, until immigration officers stamped their documents. Then, they crossed the border into the United States. Trucks took them to a processing center in Fabens, outside El Paso, to wait for American employers to arrive.

▲ Mexican workers recruited for farm work in the United States in 1943.

From the beginning, trocaderos were crowded with Mexicans who wanted to go to the United States. It soon became difficult to obtain permits to enter the program. Eventually, those who understood how the program worked learned which officials could

Patrolling the Border

Until the 1920s, Mexicans could easily enter the United States. They did not need visas or other official documents. After 1924, however, the U.S. government tightened the Mexican and Canadian borders, and crossing became more difficult.

The government tightened the borders for two reasons. One was to clamp down on alcohol smuggling. Prohibition, which began in 1920, had outlawed alcoholic beverages, but many people were still smuggling alcohol into the country. The second reason was the passage of immigration laws, in 1921 and 1924. These laws were meant to stop the large number of Asian and European immigrants coming into the United States, but they also had an effect on Mexicans crossing the border.

In 1924, Congress established the U.S. Border Patrol. Its job was to guard the Mexican and Canadian borders against alcohol smugglers and illegal immigrants. After 1924, Mexicans needed documents to enter the United States. Poor and illiterate peasants often had difficulty getting these documents. Many began to cross the border illegally in remote areas that were unguarded by the Border Patrol.

▲ Members of the Border Patrol near their cars in 1925.

"When I left, I had no idea where I was going to end up. I was thinking somebody would gets us in a car and take us over [the border]. But we had [to] walk across the desert first. I was very thirsty. We saw farmers with animals and followed them to see where they were going to drink water. It was just like little holes on the ground. And they had urine from the horses and cows. We just had to, that's how desperate you get. I was 15, I didn't think I was going to last. I'm 32 now."

Juan Ayala, 2002, describing his journey from Michoacán across the Sonoran desert in Northern Mexico. Ayala now trains horses in Kentucky.

be bribed. Many of the workers who were not chosen entered the United States illegally, beginning the first wave of illegal Mexican immigrants.

Third Wave Emigration

The bracero program ended in 1964, but the economic problems that caused so many Mexicans to emigrate continued. The earthquakes that hit central Mexico in 1985 displaced hundreds of thousands of people. Many of them moved from rural areas to northern cities near the border, where they lived a short distance from the United States. For many Mexicans, the desire to cross the border was hard to resist. Today, this temptation to cross has remained strong. The Mexican government estimates that at least three hundred and fifty thousand Mexicans per

▲ U.S. Border Patrol officers cruise the waters of the Rio Grande.

year will emigrate over the next three decades—some legally, others illegally.

In the 1990s, the U.S. government established Operation Gatekeeper, a program meant to stem the flow of illegal immigrants. As part of this program, a 14-mile (23-km) wall was built along the border between Tijuana, Mexico, and San Diego, California. The program forced many Mexicans to cross the border farther east, in the Arizona desert. Between 1995 and 2001, more than sixteen hundred people died attempting this crossing. Mexicans have also tried crossing the Rio Grande in places where U.S. agents do not patrol. In these places, the water is deeper and the currents faster. An estimated three thousand Mexicans died in the 1990s trying to cross the river.

Commuters

Some Mexicans are "commuters." They have been issued a work visa—known as a "green card"—that allows them to work legally in the United States, but they choose to keep their main home in Mexico. Commuting first began in the 1920s, and it continues today. Many commuters stay in the United States for an extended period, living and working in the country for a month or even a year and then returning to Mexico. The typical commuter, however, enters the United States in the morning and returns to Mexico at night. Under the terms of their green cards, these people should live in the United States. Few Americans complain about the arrangement, however, because the commuters spend much of their earnings on the U.S. side of the border. In addition, commuters can be hired at lower wages than American workers.

Arriving in the United States

▲ In 1948, Mexican laborers wade across the Rio Grande from Juárez, Mexico, to seek U.S. farm jobs.

The story of Mexican immigration is in many ways different from that of other immigrant groups. Long before the first wave of Mexican immigrants, the United States established borders in places where Mexicans had lived for centuries. Since the United States and Mexico shared a border, immigrants could cross back and forth many times.

These immigrants often had ties to "American" land that went back hundreds of years. Many Mexicans considered the Texas border region along the Rio Grande to be part of their homeland. Mexicans did not find much of a welcome, however, in Texas. By the early twentieth century, Mexicans who arrived in Texas often moved on to Arizona, California, and Illinois.

Early Border Violence

In the late 1800s, most Mexican immigrants crossed the Rio Grande into Texas. In this large state, they could find farm labor jobs, the main source of work for arrivals. Many immigrants, however, were

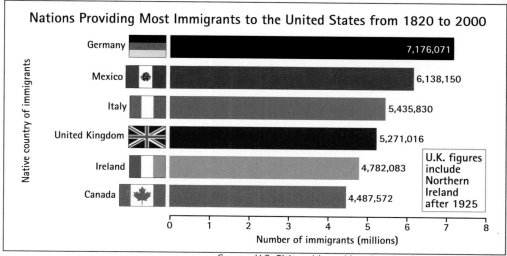

Nations Providing Most Immigrants to the United States from 1820 to 2000

Native country of immigrants	Number of immigrants
Germany	7,176,071
Mexico	6,138,150
Italy	5,435,830
United Kingdom	5,271,016
Ireland	4,782,083
Canada	4,487,572

U.K. figures include Northern Ireland after 1925

Number of immigrants (millions)

Source: U.S. Citizenship and Immigration Services, 1820–2000

▲ The nations that have provided the most immigrants to the United States are shown in this chart. More people have come from Mexico than from any other nation except Germany.

attacked by outlaw gangs. These gangs were often made up of former Confederate soldiers or their descendants. They wanted to keep Texas lands under the control of white settlers. Many white settlers considered Mexicans to be an inferior people, just as they considered Native Americans and African Americans to be inferior. They wanted to keep out or erase any traces of Mexican culture.

Mexican immigrants got little help from the police. In fact, many Mexicans believed that the Texas Rangers, the state's police force, were as dangerous as the outlaw gangs. The Rangers helped

Corridos

The dangers faced by Mexicans who immigrated to Texas in the late 1800s and early 1900s led to an important cultural development. As immigrants made their way through Texas, they heard folk songs in border towns. The songs were called *corridos*, from the Spanish word for "run." These ballads were musical communications that passed among immigrants. Some explained recent events in Texas or warned of dangers ahead. Others told of brave Mexicans who had fought the Texans. One song, "With a Pistol in His Hand," tells the story of Gregorio Cortez, a "bandit" who was said to stand up for Mexicans against the "rinches," the name given to the Texas Rangers. Another song *"Verso del mojado,"* is a story about the troubles that Mexican immigrants in Texas were likely to encounter.

maintain law and order in Texas, and they still exist today. Back then, however, Rangers often had the same racist attitudes about Mexicans as other whites. They treated Mexicans with brutality, frequently killing them.

Moving to California

Before the Border Patrol was established, in 1924, immigrants often moved back and forth between Mexico and the United States. During the Mexican Revolution, however, many new arrivals remained in the United States to avoid conflict in their homeland. They also began settling in greater numbers in California. While the conditions on California farms were often harsh, there was less anti-Mexican violence in California than in Texas.

By then, water from the Colorado River was being used to irrigate valleys in central and southern California. The state became a center of agricultural production. At the same time, refrigerated rail cars allowed crops grown in California to be shipped long distances without spoiling.

Mexicans began arriving in California just as the first U.S. immigration quotas were established by Congress. No quotas were established for countries in the Western Hemisphere; however, and an unlimited number of Mexican immigrants were allowed to enter the United States. Mexican workers soon became the chief source of farm labor for California's farmers.

◀ Bracero workers cross the border from Mexico into Hidalgo, Texas. The importance of Texas as an agricultural center faded as hundreds of thousands of farming jobs opened in California.

Segregated Barrios

For Mexican immigrants in California, life was far from ideal. Farm owners employed Mexicans because they could pay Mexican workers the same low wages they had paid to Asian laborers. Mexicans did not live in white neighborhoods. Instead, they lived in poor neighborhoods called barrios. These barrios were segregated from white communities. Aside from work, Mexicans had little contact with non-Hispanic whites, which they called "Anglos." For Mexicans arriving in the United States, the barrio was a place to find much-needed help in getting settled, but it also isolated them. For many, the crowded barrio was all they knew of their new country.

▲ The barrio home of Mexican field laborers in California in 1935. At the time, Mexicans usually lived apart from Anglos.

Settling in Other Cities

As more Mexicans arrived, many U.S. companies saw an opportunity to use them for low-cost labor in other ways besides farming. In the early 1900s, U.S. railroad companies began seeking Mexicans to lay track. The companies recruited workers in El Paso, on the border with Mexico. There, young men boarded trains to Chicago, Illinois, which was the center of the U.S. rail system.

At about the time Mexican laborers were arriving in Chicago, Americans were being called into the U.S. armed forces to fight in World War I. Many industries in Chicago had a shortage of workers. Recruiters from the city's steel mills and meat-packing industries set

⬆ U.S. railways offered Mexican workers both transportation and jobs.

up offices in El Paso as well. In 1918, the number of Mexican workers in one Chicago steel plant rose from 90 to 945. From Chicago, Mexican workers were able to use the nation's rail line to move to other cities in the Midwest and the East, such as Gary, Indiana; Akron, Ohio; and New York City.

Braceros

Mexicans who entered the United States through the bracero program found out quickly that their lives would not be easy. After arriving, the laborers usually rode in pickup trucks from farm to farm, working long hours for low pay harvesting the crops of U.S. farmers.

Although the bracero agreement stated that immigrants were to receive adequate housing and food, as well as fair wages, the program did not work as planned. Workers often had no access to bathroom facilities. In Texas, restaurants and grocery stores often refused to serve Mexicans. Conditions for immigrants in Texas became so bad that the Mexican government eventually refused to allow Mexicans to work there.

This decision, however, created another problem. Texas growers began to lure desperately poor Mexicans across the border. These

El Cortito

Workers in the bracero program often used a short-handled hoe, which they called *el cortito*, or "the short one." Using this hoe, farm workers bent over or crawled between dusty rows of plants for up to twelve hours. At the end of the day, they found it nearly impossible to stand up straight. Many workers suffered painful backaches for life. The use of the short-handle hoe is now illegal in most states, although farm workers in some areas of Texas and New Mexico still use it.

people crossed illegally into the United States by wading across the Rio Grande, earning them the insulting name "wetbacks." Illegal immigrants had first crossed the border in the 1920s. After the bracero program was established, in the 1940s, a much larger group of illegal immigrants began entering the United States.

Texas farmers liked using these immigrants because they could not complain about their working conditions. If they did, authorities would deport them to Mexico, where they faced punishment for breaking Mexican law. Farmers in Texas bribed law enforcement officials to ignore violations of the law. Illegal Mexican immigrants often had nowhere to turn for help.

▶ When Mexico did not allow bracero workers into Texas, some Mexicans worked there illegally. These illegal workers are tying up mustard greens on a Texas farm in 1948.

> "We know that we need to learn English, but somehow it just doesn't stick."
>
> *Juan Cruz, 2005. Cruz and his wife are undocumented workers in Virginia.*

Becoming Citizens

Like immigrants from other countries, Mexicans who enter the United States legally are called aliens. Although they are not U.S. citizens, they have many of the same rights as citizens.

After five consecutive years living in the United States, aliens who have entered legally can become citizens through a process called naturalization. They must be able to read and write in English and take a citizenship test. Once a person is a naturalized citizen, he or she can apply to bring family members to the United States.

Through the years, many immigrants from Mexico became naturalized, but many others did not. Some came to the United States as seasonal agricultural workers, and they returned to Mexico after working for several months. Others went back to Mexico frequently to see family members, so they could not fulfill the residency requirement.

Many of those who remained in the United States for five years generally worked and lived with other Mexican immigrants. As a result, they did not learn to speak or read English. Many immigrants had only a few years of education in Mexico. They not only had difficulty learning English, they had difficulty reading and writing Spanish.

Immigration Reform

Illegal aliens are people who have entered the United States without proper paperwork. They are also called "undocumented workers." Through the years, illegal aliens from Mexico have often remained in the United States, working in low-paying jobs. In most cases, illegal aliens cannot apply for citizenship without facing legal problems and possible deportation.

In 1986, however, Congress passed the Immigration Reform and Control Act (IRCA). One section of the act declared that illegal Mexican immigrants who had lived in the United States since 1972 without returning to Mexico could apply for citizenship. As a result of IRCA, more than two million Mexican immigrants were able to become naturalized citizens. U.S. immigration law allowed

▲ Although not yet a U.S. citizen, Manuel Mendoza fought in Iraq, where he was severely wounded. Here, he is being sworn in as a U.S. citizen in 2004.

them, as citizens, to "sponsor" family members in Mexico who wished to come to the United States. These newcomers, in turn, could apply for citizenship once they had fulfilled the necessary requirements.

Settling in New Places

In the twenty-first century, large numbers of both legal and illegal Mexican immigrants have continued to arrive in the United States. Many new arrivals have settled in places that have not traditionally had Mexican communities, such as states in the South and in the Midwest. In the South, Mexican immigrants have found work in rural areas, in poultry processing, and in light manufacturing. In Midwestern states, Mexican immigrants have taken jobs in cities, working in slaughterhouses and meat-packing plants that are near rail lines.

CHAPTER 4

History of Mexican Americans in the United States

Between 1900 and 1930, more than seven hundred thousand Mexicans legally entered the United States. Many settled in California and states in the Southwest, such as Arizona. By 1930, more than 30 percent of Mexican-born U.S. residents lived in California. People of Mexican descent—either Mexican immigrants or Mexican American citizens—made up most of the work force for large farming operations in California. At that time, people of Mexican descent called themselves Chicanos.

Growing Barrios

Thousands of newcomers made their way to cities, such as Los Angeles, California; and Tucson, Arizona. They settled in barrios

▼ A city street in East Los Angeles. By the 1930s, "East L.A." was home to thousands of Mexican Americans. It is the largest Mexican community in the United States.

East L.A.

The first settlers in Los Angeles were Mexicans. Arriving in the late 1700s, they established a mission and farmed small plots of land around the Los Angeles River. After California became a state in 1848, white settlers came to the region and forced Mexicans off their farmlands. The Mexicans then moved to the east side of the river. By 1880, East Los Angeles was the center of the Mexican American community in southern California. When the first wave of Mexican immigration began, in about 1910, "East L.A." had been home to Mexican Americans for at least 30 years.

Immigrants from Mexico were drawn to East Los Angeles for job opportunities and inexpensive housing, as well as the comfort of being surrounded by their native language and culture. In addition, East L.A. was far enough from the downtown area that immigrants felt protected from attacks by whites.

As Los Angeles grew to surround the original barrio of East L.A, immigrants continued to arrive from Mexico. By 1930, more than two hundred thousand people of Mexican descent lived in East Los Angeles. It was the largest Mexican community outside of Mexico City. Today, East L.A. is one of the oldest ethnic communities in Los Angeles. It is also the largest Mexican American community in the United States.

with U.S.-born Mexicans who could speak Spanish. The rapid increase in the population of Mexican immigrants had an impact on older Chicano communities.

Barrios were usually far from downtown—and from white neighborhoods. Railroad tracks often marked the divide between an Anglo neighborhood and a barrio, since the railways offered transportation and even work for Mexican immigrants. With the arrival of wave after wave of immigrants, the barrios themselves became divided. The poorest immigrants lived in one area of a barrio, while Mexican Americans who were better off lived in another area. No matter how successful, most Mexican Americans remained segregated from mainstream American life.

Searching for Opportunities

Although immigrants earned more money in the United States than in Mexico, they still had limited job choices. When looking for work, immigrants faced many obstacles, such as prejudice from white employers, lack of an education, and poor command of the English language. Most were forced to take low-paying, backbreaking jobs on farms and ranches and in factories.

"I am a child of Mexican immigrants from San Lucas, Michocuan. Since I was a child, I have heard stories about the journey to 'El Norte' [the North]. . . people drowned or were. . . [run] over jumping on the trains. The journey to the U.S. is something that many don't understand. Sometimes people ask why Mexicans are so devoted to their country. My answer [is] that Mexicans do not come here for pleasure but rather for a better life. My father died here very young, but this country helped my mother put us through high school and college. There is no doubt that this is the land of opportunity."

Alma Alvarez, 2002

The growth of the movie industry in southern California led to new opportunities for Mexicans. This industry created a lot of wealth in Los Angeles and surrounding areas, such as Hollywood and Beverly Hills. Mexican Americans found jobs in the service industry of southern California. They served the region's wealthy whites, working as gardeners, janitors, dish washers, and servants.

Through service jobs, Mexicans came in contact with Anglos, but they were often treated as inferiors. At the time, Mexicans faced the same prejudice and discrimination that African Americans did in the South. Mexican children went to segregated schools that were poorly funded. Zoning rules prevented Mexicans from buying homes in certain neighborhoods. Mexicans were not allowed to use community swimming pools and parks. Restaurants and movie theaters had separate sections for "white" and "colored" customers. In these cases, "colored" meant Mexican. Movies reinforced negative stereotypes of Mexicans, depicting them as bandits and lazy peasants.

As the population of Mexicans increased in California and the Southwest, many Anglos began to see the Chicano culture as a problem. School programs were developed to "Americanize" immigrant children. One program in California, for example, was called "Americanization through Homemaking." The goal of this course was to train Mexican girls to sew, cook, and clean—the very tasks that many Mexican women performed in service jobs!

Building Community

Over time, many barrios grew into strong communities. A small Chicano middle class developed in the barrios. Chicano businesses,

▲ Mexican Americans celebrate their heritage in many ways. These people are wearing traditional Mexican dress during a festival in California in 1933.

such as grocery and dry-goods stores, restaurants, barber shops, and tailor shops found customers in the barrio. Small construction firms built homes and stores. Chicanos who had finished school in Mexico or the United States taught in private Chicano schools or in segregated public schools.

In the 1920s and 1930s, people in the barrios began to form organizations called mutualistas. These groups usually met in buildings that had been bought by raising community funds. A mutualista center was part church meeting hall, part YMCA, and part welfare agency. Barrio residents gathered at these centers for funerals, weddings, baptisms, and holidays. They celebrated Mexican holidays, such as Cinco de Mayo (May 5)—the date of an important Mexican victory against French invaders—and September 16, the date of Mexico's independence from Spain. They also celebrated traditional U.S. holidays, such as the Fourth of July and Memorial Day. In addition, mutualistas provided opportunities for Mexican Americans to celebrate their culture through music and dance. Some mutualistas took the names of Mexican heroes, such as Miguel Hidalgo, who is known as the father of Mexican independence.

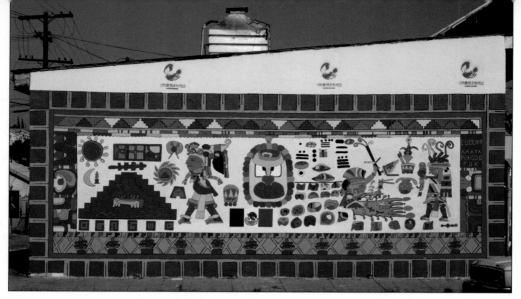

▲ This mural, in East Los Angeles, celebrates Aztec culture.

Mutualistas also helped new immigrants find housing and jobs. They provided a small amount of money for barrio families when a person was injured on a job and unable to work. In addition, they made loans to people who wanted to start small businesses but could not get loans from banks.

At mutualista centers, murals became an important cultural expression. Large murals first began to appear at these centers in the 1920s and 1930s. During that same period, Mexican artists such as Diego Rivera and José Orozco were creating massive paintings on public buildings in Mexico and in the United States. These paintings often contained scenes from Mexican history or legend. Murals became a way for artists to communicate with Mexicans both at home and in the United States. Many Mexican Americans carried on this tradition to honor the artists from their homeland and to beautify the buildings shared by their community. Over the years, these murals became an important tradition in Mexican-American communities across the country. A Mexican community center in Lincoln, Nebraska, for example, has a large mural painted by the first immigrants to the area. They had worked on railroads and in the meat-packing industries.

Repatriation

The rapid growth of Mexican American communities ended with the Great Depression of the 1930s. In addition to job losses caused by the Depression, a drought in the Midwest caused many farms to fail. Thousands of jobless migrants and landless farm families headed for California. Their need for work collided with the

▲ Conditions were often harsh for migrant farm workers and their families.
In 1937, this migrant family was living in a tiny shack at the edge of a pea field.

immigrants who were already working in the fields—Mexicans and Asians. In 1929, white laborers made up less than 20 percent of the agricultural work force in California. By 1936, white workers made up more than 85 percent of the field workers.

As the work force changed, Mexicans were accused of taking jobs from "real" Americans. Reflecting this anti-Mexican attitude, the U.S government established a repatriation program.

Under this program, the government offered free transportation back to Mexico for any Mexican who wished to leave the United States. U.S. government officials pressured Mexicans to "voluntarily" return to Mexico. During the 1930s, thousands of Mexicans were sent back. Most of these Mexicans were legal residents of the United States, and many were U.S. citizens. Some had lived in the United States for more than thirty years. In many cases, families would be broken up if the parents were aliens but their children had been born in the United States. The parents would be sent back to Mexico, but their children, as U.S. citizens, were allowed to stay.

Migrant Labor Camps

Although thousands of Mexicans left the United States during the Depression, thousands of other Mexican farm families and laborers remained in the country. With big farms cutting back on workers and hiring mainly Anglos, large numbers of Mexican migrants traveled across the Southwest looking for work.

In response to the desperate conditions faced by migrant workers, the U.S. government's Farm Security Administration (FSA) established temporary migrant labor camps. These camps provided basic shelter, food, and medicine for poverty-stricken families. The FSA actually set up several camps that were only for Mexican Americans, in order to keep them safe from anti-Mexican violence. The camps helped bring together Chicanos from separate farming regions, creating large communities.

These people had spent their lives working under extremely difficult conditions, which they had been powerless to change. They soon realized the advantage of joining together in unions to demand better working conditions and fair wages. By the mid-1930s, more than forty agricultural unions had been founded by Chicano workers in California. These unions marked the beginning of the Chicano labor movement.

The Impact of World War II

World War II changed the lives of Mexican Americans in countless ways. More than three hundred and fifty thousand Mexican Americans either volunteered or were drafted into the armed forces. They served heroically during the war. Mexican Americans had the highest proportion of Congressional Medal of Honor winners of any minority in the United States.

The war created labor shortages in defense-related industries, many of which were based in Southern California. Mexican Americans who did not serve in the armed forces suddenly found new job opportunities. Construction workers were needed to build training camps, air bases, and prisoner-of-war camps. Military supplies had to be delivered to bases. Food and textiles were needed in larger quantities. When the bracero program brought immigrants from Mexico to work on U.S. farms, Mexican Americans were needed as administrators, office workers, and interpreters for the program.

◀ Mexican-American troops training at Fort Benning, Georgia, in 1943. They got their commands twice—first in Spanish, and then in English.

By 1945, returning Mexican American veterans were no longer willing to accept their status as second-class citizens. The war created a new generation of Chicanos who were determined to make a different place for Mexican-Americans in U.S. society. The passage of the G.I. Bill helped many Mexican American veterans to achieve this goal. The act established funding for job training, college educations, and home mortgages for veterans. For the first time, Mexican Americans entered college in large numbers.

The Zoot Suit Riots

In the early 1940s, many Mexican American teenagers in Los Angeles had adopted a fashion style called "drapes." Drapes were extremely large suits, wide pants, and long coats, which were known to most Americans as "zoot suits." Young Mexican men wore these outfits when they went out at night. Many whites saw this clothing as a sign that a person belonged to a youth gang.

▲ U.S. servicemen look for anyone wearing oversize clothing, or "zoot suits," in California in 1943. They are armed with clubs, pipes, and bottles.

Los Angeles newspapers focused on the connection between people who wore zoot suits and crime in the area, which created a wave of anti-Mexican prejudice. At the time, the city was a port for U.S. servicemen leaving for duty in World War II. The mix of young men from the barrio and young men in the service exploded into violence in 1943.

On the night of June 3, eleven sailors on shore leave fought with young men who were reported later to be Mexican American "zoot suiters." The next night, more than two hundred sailors went to the Mexican American barrio in East Los Angeles. They attacked any Mexican American teenager in a zoot suit. Local police were unwilling to arrest servicemen headed to war. So, over the next two nights, other servicemen roamed through the barrio beating Mexican Americans. Barrio residents were infuriated when Los Angeles police arrested some badly beaten Mexican-American boys and charged them with causing a riot. After four days of rioting, military authorities finally declared downtown Los Angeles off limits to military personnel.

CHAPTER 5

Recent History of Mexican Americans

The 1950s and 1960s were a time of change for Mexican Americans. Many of them found jobs that were not in agriculture. In urban areas of the Southwest, Mexican communities grew. Mexican Americans who had served in the U.S. military were able to use the G.I. Bill to further their educations and purchase homes in cities.

While discrimination remained a problem, Mexican Americans began moving into middle-class occupations. Some veterans went to college to became teachers, while others received degrees in medicine, dentistry, law, and social work. A smaller number became university professors, researchers, or writers. Other veterans opened factories in cities to employ other Chicanos.

As in previous decades, however, most Chicanos were semi-skilled workers. They worked as waiters, secretaries, truckdrivers, clerks, and salespeople.

Fighting for Workers' Rights

Although the number of Mexican Americans living in urban areas grew, many Chicanos still did farm work. Thousands of migrant workers labored under difficult conditions for low wages. In decades past, some mutualistas had attempted to organize Mexican farm workers, and some local unions were formed. It was not until the 1960s, however, that Mexican labor organizations became a powerful, united force, under the leaderhip of César Chávez.

Chávez was born in Arizona, where his family ran a small store. The business failed during the Depression, and he was forced to join his parents and siblings working as a migrant laborer. In 1962,

Chávez, along with Dolores Huerta and other organizers, formed a labor group called the National Farm Workers Association (NFWA), which later turned into the United Farm Workers of America (UFW). Chávez was the main spokesperson for the UFW. The efforts of the UFW became the most widely known Mexican American movement of the time. This movement called attention to the labor issues that faced Mexican Americans and immigrants, it also created a new sense of pride in the term "Chicano."

Under Chávez, the UFW organized boycotts of products that were picked by non-union workers. A boycott of table grapes and products made from grapes, for example, lasted more than five years. It became the most successful such action in U.S. history and

▲ Labor leader César Chávez

"Operation Wetback"

In the 1950s, anti-immigrant attitudes among whites continued to cause problems for people of Mexican descent. As city barrios grew, for example, concern arose among Anglo citizens and lawmakers that many Chicanos were illegal immigrants.

In 1954, the U.S. government launched a program called "Operation Wetback". The program's insulting name was a clear indication of the long-standing prejudice faced by all Mexicans—immigrants or U.S. citizens.

Border Patrol agents, as well as state and local police, began to sweep through barrios in search of illegal immigrants. These sweeps caught not only illegal immigrants but legal immigrants and U.S. citizens as well. Although agents caught and deported more than one million illegal immigrants, they also deported immigrants' U.S.-born children, who, by law, were U.S. citizens. In addition, agents stopped "Mexican-looking" people on city streets to ask for identification, infuriating many U.S. citizens of Mexican American descent. Operation Wetback was abandoned in 1956.

forced large companies to agree to worker demands or lose millions of dollars in sales. In 1970, several large agricultural companies signed contracts that provided field workers with higher wages and better working conditions.

Mexican Pride

Chávez and other Mexican Americans helped to create the so-called Chicano Movement of the 1960s. It was a time when people of Mexican descent not only demanded equal treatment, they expressed pride in their culture—which they called Mexicanidad—through plays, film, and music. In 1965, *El Teatro Campesino* ("Farm Workers' Theater") was founded by members of the UFW. Its purpose was to perform plays based on themes that built pride in Chicano culture. El Teatro Campesino's popularity led to the founding of other "teatros" in barrios across the United States.

As these groups became more popular, they began to perform works that were written in a mix of Spanish and English for both Chicano and non-Chicano audiences. One such play was *Zoot Suit*, written by Luis Valdez in 1978. This drama about riots in Los Angeles during World War II became the first Chicano play to appear on Broadway.

Different Names, Same Heritage

Today, people of Mexican descent in the United States use different terms to refer to themselves. One of the most common is "Mexicano." In Colorado and New Mexico, "Hispano" is used, while "Tejano" is used in Texas. Mexican Americans on the West Coast may use the more general terms "Latino" or "Latin American," but Mexican Americans who have lived in California for several generations may refer to themselves as "Californios." The term "Chicano," which was used a great deal in the 1960s, is now common among younger generations. The term "Hispanic" generally refers to all Spanish-speaking people in the United States.

Barrio Gangs

One negative development in Mexican American life has been the rise of gangs in barrios. These gangs first formed in the 1940s. They arose among the children of the poorest members of the community. These people often worked in low-paying jobs that kept them away from home—and their children—for long periods of time. The children attended below-average schools and were often the victims of police brutality. Left unsupervised in the "streets," they were influenced by older youths. The gangs that formed were carried on by generations of young barrio dwellers who felt trapped in poverty and hopefulness. For these young people, a gang offered a sense of identity and belonging.

Gang members used the terms *cholos*, or "outcasts," to describe themselves. They placed the highest value on personal honor and on protecting the gang's barrios territory. Gang members dressed in specific colors and clothing styles, and they used certain signs and hand signals. In the 1980s, guns began to enter the barriors in large quantities, and conflicts between gangs turned especially violent. Drive-by shootings and other random violence affected entire neighborhoods.

▲ This young Mexican American woman is taking part in an anti-discrimination rally held in Sacramento, California, in 1971 to protest discrimination against Americans of Mexican descent.

Family and Church

Family is a very important part of Mexican American life. The Mexican family is often more than parents, children, and grandparents. It may also include uncles, aunts, and cousins, either

"I feel glad I had my quinceañera because it fulfilled not only my mother's dream, but mine as well. We were both happy that I could see myself in her eyes. To me the ceremony means that you are now more mature. You now contribute to your community."

Francisca Dionicio,
1995

by blood or by marriage. Family ties are often close. For many Mexican Americans, the welfare of the family comes before all else.

The Roman Catholic Church has also played a large role in the lives of Mexican Americans. Most Mexican Americans practice the Catholic faith, and in barrios, Catholic churches have often helped bring people together. Many traditions are tied to the Church.

Carrying on Traditions

Through the years, Mexican Americans have maintained much of their Mexican culture. One unique part of this culture is the blending together of Spanish and Native Indian traditions. Mexican Americans, for example, often mix Catholic traditions with those of their Native ancestors.

In barrios, many families observe the quinceañera. This celebration of a girl's passage

A young woman in East Los Angeles celebrates her quinceañera, which marks the passage from childhood to womanhood in Mexican culture.

▲ A boy plays a flute during the "Day of the Dead" in East Los Angeles in 2003.

to womanhood takes place when the girl turns fifteen. It began as a ceremony in the time of the Aztec empire. When Catholic priests came to Mexico, the tradition was continued, but with a Catholic focus. In Mexican American barrios, a special ceremony is held at the church, where the girl makes an offering of flowers to the Virgin Mary. After the ceremony, her family and friends enjoy a reception. This kind of party was once held in mutualista halls, but it is now usually held in a restaurant or church assembly hall.

Holidays also mix Indian and Catholic traditions. An important Mexican holiday is *El Dia de Muertos*, or "the Day of the Dead." When the Spanish conquistadors landed in Mexico, they saw that native people set aside several days in August to honor

"We not only honor our dead ancestors, we honor Mexicans killed trying to cross the border."

Arco Guerrero, 2001, an artist from Tempe, Arizona

▲ These sugar skulls have been prepared for Day of the Dead celebrations.

dead ancestors. Catholic priests tried to prevent the ceremony, but the Indians refused to stop a celebration that was thousands of years old. As a result, the priests compromised. They had the Indians move the celebration to November 1, which is known as All Souls' Day in Christian religions.

In Mexican American communities, people may celebrate by wearing wooden skull masks called *calacas*. They go to local cemeteries to decorate family grave sights with flowers and dance in honor of their deceased relatives. Sugar skulls, with the names of a dead person on the forehead, are eaten by a relative or friend. Another treat is the *pan de muerto*, or "bread of the dead." It is a round, skull-shaped sweet bread with knobs and strips of dough on top that look like skulls and bones.

Mexican Americans also celebrate *El Dia de la Virgen de Guadalupe* ("the Day of the Virgin of Guadalupe"), another holiday with Indian roots. Held on December 12, it celebrates a vision by the first Indian converted to Christianity, who is said to have seen a dark-skinned Virgin Mary in the town of Guadalupe. Since then, the Virgin of Guadalupe has been known as the patron saint of

Mexico, and she is an important symbol of strength and faith to all Mexican people.

A Mexican American home may have an *altarcito,* or "little altar." It is a blend of Indian and Mexican traditions, too. Before the Spanish arrived in Mexico, altars were found in most homes. An altarcito usually has a painting of the Virgin Mary or a favorite saint in the center. It also has items with personal meaning to the owner of the altar, usually a woman of the household. These items may include artificial flowers, stuffed animals or toys, and gifts from family members or friends. The altarcito is not a place for formal prayers, like an altar in church. Instead, it is a place where people meditate or talk to their "lucky" items in everyday language.

Speaking Spanish

Mexican Americans have maintained another part of their Mexican culture—the Spanish language. Among other immigrant groups in the United States, later generations often speak English only. Many Mexican immigrants, however, have lived in segregated barrios, and their children have attended barrio schools. Spanish has been passed down from parent to child, and people in the barrio may have few interactions with English speakers. The Mexican culture in the barrio has roots in the Spanish language. As Mexicans keep entering the country in large numbers, there is a constant flow of Spanish-speaking newcomers into the barrio.

Marrying Non-Mexicans

Mexicans in the United States have tended to marry other Mexicans. In the past, they often had no choice. As late as the 1960s, some states in the Southwest had laws against marriage between Mexicans and Anglos. In recent years, however, a fair number of Mexican Americans have married non-Mexicans. Compared to other Mexicans, they are usually better educated and more fluent in English, and they earn more money. By attending college, they meet more non-Mexican people. They tend to be a few generations removed from their immigrant ancestors.

The marriage of a Mexican American and non-Mexican can have positive and negative results. The non-Mexican spouse usually has a good education and high-paying job, too. Children from the marriage get plenty of resources to succeed. At the same time, however, these children may not have a strong connection to their Mexican culture.

CHAPTER 6

Mexican Americans in U.S. Society

I n many ways, Mexican culture has had a huge influence on American culture. This influence partly comes from the shared history of Mexico and the United States. Certain words spoken by Mexicans became part of the English language as Americans moved west—lasso, rodeo, ranch, hammock, and patio are a few examples. Many place names in the western United States come from a time when parts of the country still belonged to Spain or Mexico. The Mexican influence, however, has also come from the many immigrants who have settled in this country. Mexican Americans have made big contributions to U.S. society. They have been leaders in business, science, education, sports, and the arts.

Mexican Americans have also made their mark in politics. In 1877, Romualdo Pacheco became the first Mexican American

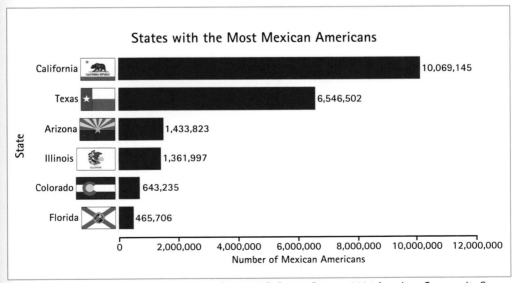

Source: U.S. Census Bureau, 2004 American Community Survey

▲ This chart shows the top six states with the most Mexican Americans.

▲ These people in New Mexico are attempting to make the world's largest enchilada.

elected to Congress, and he also served as governor of California. Since Pacheco's time, many Mexican Americans have followed in his path. Today, Mexican American Bill Richardson is the governor of New Mexico. He also served as secretary of energy under U.S. president Bill Clinton. Other Mexican Americans have been elected to local offices. Henry Cisneros, a former cabinet official under Clinton, was elected mayor of San Antonio. In 2004, voters in Los Angeles elected their first Mexican American, Antonio Villaragoso, as mayor.

Mexican Food

There is probably no part of Mexican culture that has had a greater influence on American society than food. Some elements of Mexican dishes were brought to Mexico by Spanish colonists. Other elements, however, are based on crops first grown by the Native people of Mexico, such as corn, beans, tomatoes, peppers, and avocados. Some of these crops are part of the basic American diet. Many restaurants in the country now serve Mexican dishes, and foods such as tacos, burritos, enchiladas, fajitas, tostadas, tamales, quesadillas, and salsa have become familiar to many Americans.

Making Music

Mexican Americans have made important contributions to American popular music. In the 1950s, one of the first rock and roll stars was Richard Valenzuela, better known as Ritchie Valens. His version of a traditional Mexican folk song, "*La Bamba*," became a big hit in 1957. A much bigger contribution to rock music came at the end of the sixties. In 1969, Mexican-born guitarist Carlos Santana and his band, Santana, appeared at the Woodstock Festival. Santana combined rock and blues with elements of Latin music, and he and his band became hugely popular. Even songs with Spanish lyrics and titles, such as "*Oye Como Va*" and "*Flor de Luna*," were played widely on mainstream radio stations. Today, Carlos Santana is still a popular star.

Pop singer Linda Ronstadt had many hits in the 1970s and 1980s. In the 1990s, Selena Quintanilla, a Mexican American from Corpus Christi, Texas, became a big Tejano star. Tejano is a blend of Mexican and American music that developed in barrios along the Texas border, where corridos had been sung in the early 1900s. Selena's untimely death, in 1995, was mourned by millions. The Chicano band Los Lobos, from East L.A., has also been successful with its mix of Mexican music and American rock and roll, and it scored a hit with a cover (remake) of Ritchie Valens' "*La Bamba.*"

Anti-Immigrant Attitudes

In recent years, few groups have faced more resentment from Americans than immigrants from Mexico. Much of this negative attitude is due to the fact that Mexicans continue to cross the border in large numbers. Between 1970 and 2000, the number of people of Mexican descent in the United States grew from about eight hundred thousand to nearly eight million. In 2002, a survey found that more than 30 percent of all foreign-born residents in the United States were born in Mexico. The number of illegal Mexican immigrants has caused a lot of controversy. In 2002, it was estimated that about nine million illegal immigrants lived in the country. Of these, at least five million were from Mexico.

Anti-immigration attitudes have been particularly strong in California, where politicians have often blamed economic problems on illegal immigrants. In 1994, voters passed Proposition 187, which barred illegal immigrants from schools, health clinics, and other public services. For the rest of the decade, there were several efforts to pass "English-only" laws requiring that only English be spoken in schools and workplaces. Most of these efforts failed, and Proposition 187 was eventually overturned.

▲ A Mexican immigrant family in McAllen, Texas. McAllen is in a region where Mexican and U.S. cultures often blend together.

Some people fear that "real" Americans will lose their jobs to immigrants, and they often put Mexican immigrants and Mexican American citizens in the same category. Many Mexican Americans see this attitude as a return to the days of repatriation and "Operation Wetback," when citizens as well as immigrants were sent to Mexico. They point out that many times in the past, the owners of U.S. farms and industries welcomed Mexicans because they could pay them low wages to work in horrible conditions.

Today, illegal immigration remains a controversial issue. In 2005, some members of Congress proposed laws that would deny citizenship to children born in the United States whose parents are illegal immigrants. Laws have once again been placed before

"We do the jobs that no one else wants to do . . . we pick vegetables and fruits that Americans enjoy at their tables. We are the ones who quietly wash the dishes and make sure the food is right at the table. We are the ones who make American's nights comfortable when they travel, by keeping the hotels rooms clean. We make Americans feel comfortable at home by being gardeners, house cleaners, and baby sitters. We are the silent ghosts who give America comfort."

Salvatore Barrio, 2003. Barrio is a legal Mexican immigrant.

These high school students in Los Angeles are marching to a rally held in 2006 to protest proposed anti-immigration laws. Some are waving Mexican flags.

voters in California that would deny government benefits to those who cannot prove they have immigrated legally. Other laws would cut off benefits to all non-citizens, including legal immigrants.

Mexican American leaders point out that U.S. lawmakers are often willing to take a hard line against immigrants to win favor with voters. They also note that U.S. employers who hire illegal immigrants are rarely punished. The solution to illegal immigration, they say, does not lie at the border. Instead, illegal immigration would be reduced if the U.S. government enforced laws for providing decent wages and working conditions. Industries would then have less reason to hire illegal immigrants who would not complain about the work they did.

Breaking Down Barriers

Many Mexican-Americans have now moved up the economic ladder. They have also gained a stronger political voice. People of Mexican descent, however, still have barriers to overcome in trying to find better opportunities. One barrier is language. Compared to immigrants from Asia or Europe, Mexicans are much closer to their homeland. They have stayed connected

> "If you go after labor law violations, which the government has never done, that is when you start to eliminate the job market for undocumented labor. This would also mean that legal immigrants and citizens would be treated fairly."
>
> *Cecilia Muñoz, 1998. Muñoz is vice president of the National Council of La Raza (NCLR), an organization that represents Mexican Americans*

to its people and culture, including its language. In barrios, people often speak Spanish, and it can be hard to learn English in this environment. Mexican American leaders say that many immigrants have not taken the steps needed to become U.S. citizens—and get the right to vote—because they do not know English. "Latinos can exist in their own community and never have to learn English," says Texas congressman Charles Gonzalez. "My fear is that we have not only isolated ourselves, but we have handicapped ourselves."

No matter what the future holds, people of Mexican descent will continue meeting new challenges, and they will continue making important contributions to U.S. society. They have already shown what their determination and hard work can accomplish in the face of great obstacles.

"When I came to the United States, I was very proud of who I was. I was a Mexican. I had an identity. I had been taught a history, a culture of centuries of rich civilization. I grew up in a very happy environment but a very poor environment."

Antonia Hernández, 2002. Hernández, a lawyer for Chicano civil rights organizations, immigrated to California as a child in the early 1950s.

"Amexica"

In Texas's Rio Grande Valley, there is a region that many people call "Amexica." In this region along the Mexican border, Mexican and U.S. cultures have blended together. Amexica stretches from El Paso to McAllen, Texas. McAllen and Laredo, Texas, another city in this region, are among the fastest-growing cities in the United States. Each day, more than eight hundred thousand Mexicans cross legally from Mexico into these cities to work as dishwashers, maids, gardeners, carpenters, and health-care workers. An estimated forty-five hundred cross illegally every day. In these cities, workers earn more in one hour than they would earn in an entire day in Mexico. Many who cross the border decide to remain in the United States.

The culture of this borderland is reflected in the mixed Spanish and English language—called Spanglish—that is spoken on the streets and appears on signs. Spanish language newspapers, radio stations, and TV networks are part of the border culture. A blend of country music and Mexican music, called "Tex-Mex," is one of the most popular styles in the area.

"Today the border is not where the U.S. stops and Mexico begins," says Laredo mayor Betty Flores, a Mexican American. "It's where the U.S. blends into Mexico."

Notable Mexican Americans

Baez, Joan (1941–) U.S.-born folk singer who became famous in the 1960s for both her music and her political activism.

Cisneros, Sandra (1954–) U.S.-born writer who is the author of *House on Mango Street* (1984), an acclaimed novel about a Mexican American girl growing up in Chicago.

De La Hoya, Oscar (1973–) U.S.-born boxer who won an Olympic gold medal (1992) and professional championships in five different weight classes.

Huerta, Dolores C. (1930–) U.S.-born labor leader and co-founder of the National Farm Workers Association (NFWA); it later became the United Farm Workers of America (UFW).

Galarza, Ernesto (1905–1984) Mexican-born professor, author, and labor leader, and the first Mexican American to be nominated for the Nobel Prize for Literature.

Gonzalez, Ricardo "Pancho" (1928–1995) U.S.-born tennis champion, member of Tennis Hall of Fame.

Ochoa, Ellen (1958–) U.S.-born physicist and astronaut who has been on four space shuttle flights.

Olmos, Edward James (1947–) U.S.-born actor who appeared in the play *Zoot Suit* on Broadway and was nominated for an Academy Award in the film *Stand and Deliver*, for his portrayal of a math teacher in a barrio high school. He was also a featured regular on the hit TV series *Miami Vice* and *Hill Street Blues*.

Roybal-Allard, Lucille (1943–) U.S.-born congressional representative from California; became the first Mexican American woman to be elected to the U.S. Congress, in 1993.

Valens, Ritchie (1941–1959) U.S.-born singer who became one of the early stars of rock and roll; along with Buddy Holly and the "Big Bopper," he was killed in a plane crash in 1959.

Villa-Komaroff, Lydia (1947–) U.S.-born biologist, founding member of the Society for the Advancement of Chicanos and Native Americans in Science.

Time Line

1521 Spain establishes colony in Mexico.

1821 Mexico wins independence from Spain. It allows Stephen F. Austin to begin Texas colonization.

1836 Texas wins independence from Mexico.

1846 The Mexican American War begins.

1848 Gold is discovered in the Sacramento Valley area of California. Large numbers of U.S. pioneers and immigrants from around the world begin traveling to the area. Many gold seekers set up camps on Mexican-held land, forcing out some of the original landowners.

1848 The Treaty of Guadalupe Hidalgo ends the Mexican American War.

1910 Mexican Revolution begins, causing hundreds of thousands of Mexicans to enter the United States to escape conflict.

1924 Immigration Act of 1924 halts the flow of immigrant groups from many parts of the world. Largely due to a lack of immigration quotas in the Western Hemisphere, more than 89,000 Mexicans come into the United States on permanent visas. U.S. Border Patrol is created to monitor the borders of the United States.

1942 The bracero program begins, allowing Mexicans to work temporarily in the United States, mostly in agriculture.

1962 César Chávez, Dolores Huerta, and others organize the National Farm Workers Association (NFWA) in Delano, California.

1964 Bracero program ends.

1965 Hart-Celler Immigration Act is passed by Congress. It increases immigration from most countries but limits the legal immigration of Mexicans.

1986 Congress passes the Immigration Reform and Control Act (IRCA). A section of the act allows Mexican immigrants who have lived in the United States illegally since 1972 to become legal.

1990 Immigration Act increases the total immigration quota to seven hundred thousand per year.

1996 U.S. Border Patrol installs sensors and a fence along the border between California and Mexico to prevent illegal immigrants from entering the United States.

2000 Los Angeles voters elect the city's first Mexican American mayor.

2006 New proposed immigration laws lead to large protest demonstrations across the country by Mexicans, other immigrants, and U.S. citizens.

Glossary

aliens people living in a nation that is not their original homeland, who have not become citizens of their new nation of residence

Anglo term used to describe non-Hispanic whites

barrio a section of a city or town where Spanish-speaking people, such as Mexican immigrants and Mexican Americans, live.

boycott refusal by a group to buy certain goods or shop in certain stores

Chicano a name that has sometimes been used by Mexican Americans and immigrants to refer to themselves

colony nation, territory, or people under the control of another country

conquistadors Spanish word for conqueror; usually refers to Spanish explorers who conquered the Americas in the 1500s

criollos people of purely Spanish descent born in Mexico

culture language, beliefs, customs, and ways of life shared by a group of people from the same region or nation

deport force a non-citizen to return to the person's country of origin

discrimination negative treatment of a certain group of people

drought a prolonged period with little or no rain

emigrate leave one nation or region to go live in another place

ethnic having to do with a group of people of the same race, culture, religion, or place of origin

fluent able to speak a language easily and well

G.I. Bill law that gave low-cost loans for housing and college to U.S. soldiers who served during World War II

heritage cultural tradition handed down from generation to generation

illiterate not able to read and write

immigration the act of coming to a new country to live there

mestizos people of mixed Spanish and Indian descent

migrants people who move regularly from one area to another in order to find work, especially in agriculture

missions places established for the purpose of spreading a religion

prejudice bias against, or dislike of, a person or group because of race, nationality, religion, or other factors

quota a limit on the number of something, such as the number of immigrants from a particular country allowed into the United States

racist having to do with prejudice toward a particular race of people

repatriation the act of returning to the country of one's origin after living in another country

segregated kept apart or separate from other groups

service industry businesses that provide a service to people

stereotype an image, often incorrect, that people have of a certain group

third generation the grandchildren of immigrants' U.S.-born children

visas document that permits a person to enter a nation for a set period of time

Further Resources

Books

Bloom, Barbara Lee. *The Mexican Americans*. Immigrants in America (series).
    Lucent Books (2003).
Brown, Jonatha A. *César Chávez*. Trailblazers of the Modern World (series).
    World Almanac Library (2004).
Doering, Amanda. *Cinco de Mayo: Day of Mexican Pride*.
    First Facts Books (2006).
Tidmarsh, Celia. *Focus on Mexico*. World in Focus (series).
    Gareth Stevens (2006).

Web Sites

The New Frontier
www.time.com/time/covers/1101010611/
Surf *TIME* Magazine's report on the latest in Mexican immigrant experiences.

The Borderlands Encyclopedia
www.utep.edu/border/
Follow links to a variety of informational topics concerning
the Mexican American immigrant experience.

Publisher's note to educators and parents: Our editors have carefully reviewed these Web sites to ensure that they are suitable for children. Many Web sites change frequently, however, and we cannot guarantee that a site's future contents will continue to meet our high standards of quality and educational value. Be advised that children should be closely supervised whenever they access the Internet.

Where to Visit

The Alamo
300 Alamo Plaza
San Antonio TX 78299
www.thealamo.org

About the Author

Scott Ingram is the author of more than fifty books for young adults. In 2004, he won the NAACP Image Award for an outstanding literary work for children for his book about the Civil Rights March of 1963, published by World Almanac® Library in its *Landmark Events in American History* series. Ingram lives in Portland, Connecticut.

Index

2160800166

973
ING

Ingram, Scott.

Mexican Americans

$18.56

DATE DUE	BORROWER'S NAME	ROOM NO.
11/8/12	Miguel Zavaleta	

2160800166

973
ING

Ingram, Scott.

Mexican Americans

HORACE FURNESS HIGH SCHOOL
SCHOOL DISTRICT OF PHILA

428781 01856   22780A   0006